Designing Effective Instruction - A Comprehensive Guide to the Kirkpatrick Model

"Unlocking Learning Excellence: Empowering Minds for Success"

Apurva Roy

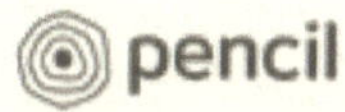

ISBN 978-93-5883-088-0
© Apurva Roy 2023

Published in India 2023 by Pencil

A brand of
One Point Six Technologies Pvt. Ltd.
Unit no. 26, Ground Floor, Building A1,
Wadala Truck Terminal Road,
Near Post Office, Antop Hill, Mumbai - 400037
E connect@thepencilapp.com
W www.thepencilapp.com

Author biography

Apurva Roy is a passionate educator and instructional designer dedicated to transforming the landscape of learning and development. With a background in education and a keen interest in technology, Apurva specializes in creating engaging and impactful learning experiences that empower individuals to reach their full potential.

As the author of this book, Apurva draws upon years of experience in the field of instructional design and training evaluation. Through extensive research and practical application, Apurva has honed a deep understanding of the Kirkpatrick Model and its significance in measuring training effectiveness.

Driven by a belief in the power of continuous improvement, Apurva emphasizes the value of data-driven decision-making and the integration of emerging technologies to revolutionize the world of training and development. Their passion for creating learner-centric experiences has led them to explore innovative trends, such as XR, AI-powered personalization, and gamification.

Apurva's commitment to excellence is reflected in their dedication to fostering collaborative learning communities and nurturing a growth mindset among learners and organizations alike. Their work seeks to bridge the gap between theory and practice, ensuring that training initiatives result in tangible improvements and positive organizational outcomes.

Beyond their writing and instructional design endeavors, Apurva remains committed to sharing knowledge, promoting best practices, and inspiring others to embrace the transformative potential of training and development. Their vision is to empower organizations to create a skilled and thriving workforce capable of meeting the challenges of the future with confidence and competence.

Through this book and their broader contributions to the field, Apurva aims to spark a journey of continuous learning and innovation, paving the way for a brighter and more knowledgeable tomorrow.

CONTENTS

Introduction

Welcome to "Designing Effective Instruction: A Comprehensive Guide to the Kirkpatrick Model." This book aims to provide educators, trainers, instructional designers, and anyone involved in the field of learning and development with a thorough understanding of the renowned Kirkpatrick Model and its practical application in various training programs.

In today's fast-paced world, organizations invest significant resources in employee training and development to stay competitive and foster growth. However, ensuring that these training initiatives yield tangible results can be a challenge. This is where the Kirkpatrick Model comes into play—a robust evaluation framework that helps assess training effectiveness and measure the impact of learning on both individuals and organizations.

This book is structured to guide you through each level of the Kirkpatrick Model, starting from capturing initial learner reactions to evaluating the ultimate impact on the organization. You will learn how to design training programs that align with organizational objectives, effectively measure learning outcomes, and continuously improve the training process.

Throughout the chapters, we will explore real-world case studies that illustrate the successful implementation of the Kirkpatrick Model in various contexts. These case studies will highlight how organizations have leveraged the model to optimize their training efforts, enhance employee performance, and drive business success.

Whether you are a seasoned instructional designer seeking to refine your evaluation strategies or a novice trainer looking to understand how to assess the effectiveness of your programs, this book has something valuable to offer. By the end of this journey, you will possess the knowledge and tools necessary to become a proficient practitioner of instructional design, armed with the ability to create impactful learning experiences that lead to tangible and measurable results.

Let's embark on this enlightening journey into the world of instructional design and the Kirkpatrick Model.

Chapter 1 - Introduction to Instructional Design

Instructional design serves as the cornerstone of any successful training program. In this chapter, we embark on a journey into the world of instructional design, exploring its purpose, principles, and process in-depth. By the end of this chapter, you will gain a comprehensive understanding of the key elements that contribute to designing effective instruction.

1.1 The Significance of Instructional Design

Before diving into the intricacies of instructional design, let's take a moment to recognize its significance in the realm of learning and development. Instructional design is not a mere afterthought; rather, it is a deliberate and systematic approach to crafting learning experiences that lead to meaningful outcomes. Its core objective is to align training initiatives with specific learning objectives and organizational goals.

The process of instructional design is rooted in research-based methodologies and is driven by data and analysis. By adopting an evidence-based approach, instructional designers can create targeted and tailored learning experiences that cater to the diverse needs of learners.

1.2 Understanding the Learners

At the heart of instructional design are the learners—the individuals who will participate in the training program. Understanding their characteristics, needs, and preferences is paramount to crafting effective instruction. Factors such as age, educational background, prior knowledge, and learning styles all play a crucial role in designing engaging and impactful learning experiences.

Conducting a thorough needs analysis is an essential first step in this process. By gathering information about the learners' existing knowledge gaps and identifying their learning objectives, instructional designers can tailor the content and delivery to suit their audience accurately.

1.3 Defining Clear Learning Objectives

Learning objectives serve as guideposts for both learners and instructors. They articulate the intended outcomes of the training program and provide a clear roadmap for the learning journey. Well-defined learning objectives are specific, measurable, achievable, relevant, and time-bound (SMART), making it easier to assess learners' progress and the overall effectiveness of the instruction.

In this section, we will explore various taxonomies and frameworks used to define learning objectives, such as Bloom's Taxonomy, which categorizes learning objectives into cognitive domains ranging from simple recall of information to complex application and evaluation of knowledge.

1.4 Selecting Appropriate Instructional Strategies

Once learning objectives are established, the next step is to determine the most suitable instructional strategies to achieve those objectives. Instructional strategies encompass a wide range of approaches, including lectures, discussions, hands-on activities, simulations, and multimedia presentations.

The choice of instructional strategies depends on factors such as the content complexity, the nature of the subject matter, the available resources, and the learners' preferences. A well-balanced mix of instructional methods can enhance engagement and knowledge retention among learners.

1.5 Designing and Developing Learning Materials

With learning objectives defined and instructional strategies selected, the focus shifts to creating the actual learning materials. This may include designing presentations, developing e-learning modules, curating relevant reading materials, and preparing assessment tools.

The design of learning materials should be visually appealing, accessible, and aligned with the overall instructional design plan. Additionally, incorporating interactive elements and multimedia can make the learning experience more dynamic and immersive.

1.6 Implementing and Evaluating Instruction

The implementation phase marks the actual delivery of the training program to the learners. During this stage, instructors or trainers play a crucial role in facilitating the learning process, ensuring that learners have access to the designed materials and guidance to achieve their learning objectives.

Simultaneously, ongoing evaluation is an integral part of the instructional design process. Formative assessments, feedback sessions, and learner surveys can provide valuable insights into the effectiveness of the instruction and help identify areas for improvement.

1.7 Conclusion

In conclusion, instructional design forms the backbone of successful training programs. By considering the learners' needs, defining clear objectives, selecting appropriate strategies, and developing engaging learning materials, instructional designers can create transformative learning experiences that drive individual growth and contribute to organizational success.

In the following chapters, we will delve deeper into the intricacies of the Kirkpatrick Model and its role in evaluating the effectiveness of instructional design. So, let us proceed on this enlightening journey into the world of instructional design and evaluation.

Chapter 2 - Understanding the Kirkpatrick Model

In Chapter 1, we explored the fundamentals of instructional design. Now, in Chapter 2, we turn our focus to the renowned Kirkpatrick Model, a comprehensive framework for evaluating training effectiveness. Developed by Dr. Donald L. Kirkpatrick in the late 1950s, this model has become a cornerstone of learning and development evaluation. By the end of this chapter, you will gain a deep understanding of the Kirkpatrick Model's four levels of evaluation.

2.1 The Origins of the Kirkpatrick Model

Before delving into the four levels of evaluation, let's briefly discuss the origins of the Kirkpatrick Model. Dr. Donald L. Kirkpatrick, a prominent educator and researcher, first introduced this model in his doctoral dissertation in 1954. Over time, the model evolved and gained widespread recognition in the field of instructional design.

The Kirkpatrick Model is known for its practicality and adaptability across various training contexts, making it a valuable tool for organizations seeking to measure the impact of their learning initiatives.

2.2 Level 1: Reaction - Capturing Learner Feedback

The first level of the Kirkpatrick Model focuses on capturing learners' reactions to the training experience. It involves collecting feedback from participants regarding their perceptions of the training program, including aspects such as the training content, delivery methods, and instructor effectiveness.

Feedback at this level is typically gathered through surveys, questionnaires, or focus group discussions. Understanding learners' reactions is crucial as it provides insights into their engagement, satisfaction, and perceived relevance of the training. Positive reactions can lead to increased motivation and willingness to participate actively in the learning process.

2.3 Level 2: Learning - Assessing Knowledge and Skill Acquisition

Moving beyond learner reactions, Level 2 of the Kirkpatrick Model aims to assess the extent to which participants have acquired new knowledge and skills. This evaluation focuses on the learning outcomes and measures the learners' comprehension, retention, and application of the content.

Various assessment methods, such as quizzes, tests, practical exercises, and simulations, can be used to gauge the level of learning achieved. The results from Level 2 evaluation provide valuable feedback on the effectiveness of the instructional design and the clarity of the learning objectives.

2.4 Level 3: Behavior - Measuring Application of Learning

Level 3 evaluation shifts the focus from what learners know to how they apply their knowledge and skills in real-world settings. This level assesses the extent to which participants have transferred their learning to their job roles or daily activities.

Measuring behavior change can be more complex than assessing learning, as it often requires observation or self-reporting of changes in on-the-job performance. However, Level 3 evaluation is crucial in determining the practical impact of the training and its effectiveness in influencing behavior change.

2.5 Level 4: Results - Evaluating Organizational Impact

The ultimate goal of any training program is to deliver tangible results that positively impact the organization. Level 4 of the Kirkpatrick Model evaluates the broader organizational outcomes resulting from the training.

This evaluation involves analyzing key performance indicators (KPIs), business metrics, and other relevant data to assess the training's impact on productivity, efficiency, cost savings, and other organizational goals. Level 4 evaluation helps determine the return on investment (ROI) of the training and its overall contribution to the organization's success.

2.6 Applying the Kirkpatrick Model Effectively

While each level of the Kirkpatrick Model provides valuable insights, it is essential to apply the model effectively to derive meaningful conclusions. Integrating evaluation plans from the initial stages of instructional design, aligning evaluation metrics with learning objectives, and using a combination of qualitative and quantitative data collection methods are some key strategies for successful application.

Conclusion:

Understanding the four levels of the Kirkpatrick Model lays the foundation for comprehensive training evaluation. By systematically assessing learners' reactions, learning outcomes, behavior change, and organizational impact, organizations can optimize their training programs to drive continuous improvement and achieve measurable results.

In the subsequent chapters, we will explore each level in greater detail and examine real-world case studies showcasing the successful implementation of the Kirkpatrick Model in various instructional design scenarios. Let us proceed with our exploration of this invaluable model.

Chapter 3 - The Four Levels of the Kirkpatrick Model

In Chapter 2, we gained an overview of the Kirkpatrick Model and its significance in evaluating training effectiveness. Now, in Chapter 3, we delve deeper into each of the four levels of the model, exploring their methodologies and importance in measuring the impact of training programs.

3.1 Level 1: Reaction - Capturing Learner Feedback

At Level 1, the focus is on capturing learners' reactions to the training experience. This level addresses the question, "Did the learners find the training engaging and relevant?" To gather feedback, organizations can use post-training surveys, questionnaires, or focus group discussions. These tools provide learners with an opportunity to express their opinions on various aspects of the training, such as the course content, delivery methods, and the effectiveness of the instructor.

While Level 1 evaluation is often the simplest to implement, it is essential in understanding learners' initial impressions of the training. Positive reactions foster a favorable learning environment, leading to higher engagement and motivation. However, it is important to note that Level 1 evaluation is just the beginning, and its outcomes alone do not fully assess the training's effectiveness.

3.2 Level 2: Learning - Assessing Knowledge and Skill Acquisition

Level 2 evaluation aims to assess the degree of knowledge and skills acquired by learners during the training program. The question addressed at this level is, "Did the learners gain the intended knowledge and skills?" To measure learning outcomes effectively, instructional designers can employ various assessment methods, such as quizzes, tests, assignments, and practical demonstrations.

The results from Level 2 evaluation provide valuable insights into the training's effectiveness in achieving the desired learning objectives. It helps identify areas where learners may need additional support or where the instructional design can be enhanced for better knowledge retention and skill development.

3.3 Level 3: Behavior - Measuring Application of Learning

Moving beyond assessing what learners have learned, Level 3 evaluation focuses on measuring the application of newly acquired knowledge and skills in the workplace or real-life settings. The central question at this level is, "Are learners applying what they learned on the job?"

Level 3 evaluation can be more challenging to execute, as it often requires observation, performance assessments, or self-reports from learners and their supervisors. However, understanding the practical impact of training on learners' behavior and job performance is crucial in determining the training's effectiveness in driving real-world results.

3.4 Level 4: Results - Evaluating Organizational Impact

Level 4 evaluation is the pinnacle of the Kirkpatrick Model, addressing the ultimate question, "What is the organizational impact of the training?" At this level, organizations analyze the training's contribution to broader business outcomes and key performance indicators (KPIs).

To evaluate organizational impact, organizations can analyze data on factors such as productivity, cost savings, revenue growth, customer satisfaction, and employee retention. The goal is to determine the return on investment (ROI) of the training and assess its overall influence on the organization's success.

3.5 The Interconnectedness of the Levels

One crucial aspect to acknowledge is the interconnectedness of the four levels. The success of Level 4 evaluation, measuring organizational impact, is built upon the foundation laid by the preceding levels. Positive reactions (Level 1), successful learning outcomes (Level 2), and behavior change (Level 3) are all instrumental in achieving meaningful organizational results.

By systematically evaluating each level, organizations can gain a comprehensive understanding of the effectiveness of their training programs. Additionally, the data collected from the evaluation process helps identify areas for improvement and guides decision-making in future instructional design efforts.

3.6 Conclusion

In conclusion, the Kirkpatrick Model provides a robust and practical framework for evaluating training effectiveness. Each level of the model contributes unique insights, ultimately guiding organizations in optimizing their training initiatives to drive enhanced learning outcomes and positive organizational impact.

In the subsequent chapters, we will delve into real-world case studies showcasing the successful application of the Kirkpatrick Model in instructional design scenarios. So, let us continue our exploration of this invaluable model and uncover its potential to transform learning and development practices.

Chapter 4 - Real-World Case Studies of the Kirkpatrick Model in Instructional Design

In Chapter 3, we explored the four levels of the Kirkpatrick Model and their significance in evaluating training effectiveness. Now, in Chapter 4, we will delve into real-world case studies showcasing the successful application of the Kirkpatrick Model in various instructional design scenarios.

4.1 Case Study 1: "Tech Solutions Inc. - Onboarding Program"

Background: Tech Solutions Inc., a rapidly growing technology firm, recognized the importance of a robust onboarding program to ensure new employees quickly assimilate into their roles and contribute to the organization's success. The HR and Learning & Development teams collaborated to design a comprehensive onboarding program, leveraging the Kirkpatrick Model for evaluation.

Application of the Kirkpatrick Model:

Level 1 (Reaction): After each onboarding session, new employees were asked to complete a feedback survey. The positive responses indicated that the program's content and delivery were engaging and relevant. Participants appreciated the interactive elements and the opportunity to connect with their peers.

Level 2 (Learning): To assess learning outcomes, participants were given knowledge assessments at the end of the onboarding period. The results demonstrated that the employees had acquired a solid understanding of the company's mission, values, and their specific job roles.

Level 3 (Behavior): Tech Solutions Inc. monitored new employees' progress during their initial months on the job. Supervisors observed that the onboarding program had a positive impact on employees' confidence and performance, leading to faster integration into their teams.

Level 4 (Results): Evaluating the program's organizational impact, the company observed a reduction in the time it took for new employees to reach full productivity. This, in turn, contributed to improved team performance and overall efficiency, leading to cost savings and increased customer satisfaction.

4.2 Case Study 2: "HealthCare Academy - Patient Care Training"

Background: HealthCare Academy, a renowned healthcare institution, aimed to enhance patient care by improving the skills and knowledge of their nursing staff. The Training and Development department devised a patient care training program with the Kirkpatrick Model as the evaluation framework.

Application of the Kirkpatrick Model:

Level 1 (Reaction): Feedback forms were distributed among nursing staff after each training session. The majority of participants expressed high satisfaction with the program, stating that the training materials were informative and relevant to their daily responsibilities.

Level 2 (Learning): Pre and post-training assessments were conducted to measure the increase in medical knowledge and patient care skills. The results showed a significant improvement in areas such as critical thinking, patient communication, and clinical procedures.

Level 3 (Behavior): Observations and patient feedback were used to assess behavioral changes in nursing staff. The training led to more empathetic patient interactions and a reduction in medical errors, enhancing the overall quality of care.

Level 4 (Results): Analyzing patient satisfaction scores and healthcare outcomes, HealthCare Academy found that the patient care training positively impacted patient experience, leading to increased patient trust and higher rates of patient referrals.

4.3 Case Study 3: "Financial Excellence Institute - Leadership Development"

Background: The Financial Excellence Institute recognized the need to cultivate strong leadership within their organization. They designed a leadership development program, integrating the Kirkpatrick Model to measure its effectiveness.

Application of the Kirkpatrick Model:

Level 1 (Reaction): Participant feedback was collected through surveys after each leadership training module. The program received positive reviews for its engaging workshops, insightful discussions, and expert facilitators.

Level 2 (Learning): Pre and post-training assessments evaluated participants' leadership competencies. The results revealed a notable improvement in areas such as decision-making, communication, and team-building skills.

Level 3 (Behavior): A 360-degree feedback process was implemented to assess changes in leadership behavior. Colleagues and subordinates reported a significant increase in the effectiveness of leaders in motivating and guiding their teams.

Level 4 (Results): Evaluating the program's impact on the organization, the Financial Excellence Institute observed improved employee engagement, reduced turnover rates, and increased profitability, all attributed to the enhanced leadership capabilities of the participants.

4.4 Conclusion

These case studies demonstrate the practical application of the Kirkpatrick Model in diverse instructional design scenarios. By using the model's four levels of evaluation, organizations gain valuable insights into the effectiveness of their training programs and their impact on learners and the organization as a whole.

The Kirkpatrick Model's versatility and adaptability make it an indispensable tool for continuous improvement and evidence-based decision-making in the field of learning and development. As we proceed further in this book, we will continue to explore best practices and real-world examples that showcase how organizations can leverage this model to create impactful and transformative learning experiences.

Chapter 5 - Best Practices in Leveraging the Kirkpatrick Model for Training Optimization

In Chapter 4, we explored real-world case studies highlighting the successful application of the Kirkpatrick Model in instructional design scenarios. Now, in Chapter 5, we will delve into best practices for organizations to effectively leverage the Kirkpatrick Model to optimize their training programs and drive meaningful learning outcomes.

5.1 Begin with Clear and Measurable Learning Objectives

The foundation of effective training evaluation lies in well-defined and measurable learning objectives. Before designing any training program, instructional designers must collaborate with stakeholders to establish specific and achievable learning goals. Clear learning objectives serve as guideposts throughout the instructional design process and provide a basis for evaluating the training's success at Level 2 (Learning) of the Kirkpatrick Model.

5.2 Align Evaluation Metrics with Learning Objectives

To ensure a comprehensive evaluation, organizations should align their evaluation metrics with the established learning objectives. Each level of the Kirkpatrick Model should focus on assessing the intended outcomes of the training. For example, if the learning objective is to improve customer service skills, evaluation at Level 3 (Behavior) should gauge how well employees apply these skills in real-life customer interactions.

5.3 Incorporate Multiple Data Collection Methods

Gathering diverse and meaningful data is essential for accurate training evaluation. Organizations should employ a mix of quantitative and qualitative data collection methods. Quantitative data, such as assessments and surveys, offer measurable results, while qualitative data, including focus groups and interviews, provide valuable insights into learners' experiences and behavior changes.

5.4 Implement Evaluation Throughout the Training Process

Integrating evaluation throughout the training process ensures continuous improvement and timely feedback. Rather than waiting until the end of the program, consider conducting formative assessments at strategic points during the training. This ongoing evaluation helps identify any issues early on and allows for adjustments to be made to enhance the learning experience.

5.5 Involve Stakeholders and Learners

Stakeholder engagement is vital for successful training evaluation. Involve key stakeholders, such as senior management, supervisors, and learners themselves, in the evaluation process. Their input and perspectives provide a holistic view of the training's impact and contribute to evidence-based decision-making.

5.6 Use Technology to Facilitate Evaluation

Incorporating technology into the evaluation process streamlines data collection and analysis. Learning management systems (LMS) and survey tools make it easier to administer assessments and gather feedback. Additionally, data analytics tools can provide valuable insights into learner progress and performance.

5.7 Analyze and Act on Evaluation Results

The value of training evaluation lies in its ability to drive improvement. Analyze the evaluation results carefully and identify areas of strength and areas for enhancement. Use this information to inform future instructional design decisions and fine-tune training programs for better outcomes.

5.8 Emphasize the Value of Evaluation to Stakeholders

Lastly, emphasize the value of training evaluation to stakeholders. Demonstrating the positive impact of training on learners' skills, behavior, and organizational results reinforces the importance of continued investment in employee development. Showcase the ROI of training initiatives to garner support for future learning and development endeavors.

5.9 Conclusion

Effectively leveraging the Kirkpatrick Model for training optimization is a dynamic process that requires deliberate planning, stakeholder involvement, and a commitment to continuous improvement. By following these best practices, organizations can harness the power of the Kirkpatrick Model to create impactful learning experiences, improve performance outcomes, and achieve organizational success.

In the following chapters, we will delve deeper into specific aspects of instructional design, exploring topics such as enhancing training through technology, designing engaging learning experiences, and addressing challenges in implementing the Kirkpatrick Model. Let us continue our journey of unlocking the full potential of instructional design and evaluation.

Chapter 6 - Enhancing Training Effectiveness through Technology

In Chapter 5, we explored best practices for leveraging the Kirkpatrick Model to optimize training programs. Now, in Chapter 6, we will delve into the role of technology in enhancing training effectiveness. In today's digital age, technology offers a plethora of tools and platforms that can transform the learning experience and streamline the evaluation process.

6.1 Learning Management Systems (LMS)

Learning Management Systems (LMS) serve as centralized platforms to manage and deliver training content. LMS enables organizations to organize courses, track learners' progress, and administer assessments efficiently. By using an LMS, organizations can collect valuable data on learners' interactions with the training material, allowing for more comprehensive evaluation at all levels of the Kirkpatrick Model.

6.2 Interactive E-Learning Modules

Interactive e-learning modules go beyond traditional lecture-style training by incorporating multimedia elements, quizzes, simulations, and gamification. These modules engage learners and foster active participation, leading to better knowledge retention. Interactive e-learning also provides real-time feedback to learners, enabling them to gauge their progress and identify areas for improvement.

6.3 Virtual Reality (VR) and Augmented Reality (AR)

Virtual Reality (VR) and Augmented Reality (AR) technologies offer immersive learning experiences that simulate real-life scenarios. These technologies are particularly valuable in fields where hands-on training is essential, such as medical simulations or equipment operation. VR and AR training can be used to assess learners' skills (Level 2) and behavior (Level 3) in realistic and safe environments.

6.4 Mobile Learning

Mobile learning, or m-learning, allows learners to access training content on their smartphones or tablets anytime, anywhere. This flexibility is especially beneficial for learners with busy schedules or remote work arrangements. M-learning applications can also incorporate microlearning, delivering bite-sized content that learners can easily consume and retain.

6.5 Data Analytics for Evaluation

Technology enables the collection and analysis of vast amounts of training data. Data analytics tools can process this information and generate actionable insights. Organizations can use data analytics to identify trends, measure the effectiveness of training interventions, and make data-driven decisions to improve training outcomes.

6.6 Personalized Learning Paths

With technology, organizations can offer personalized learning paths to cater to individual learner needs and preferences. Adaptive learning platforms use data to deliver customized content and assessments based on each learner's strengths and weaknesses. Personalized learning enhances engagement and ensures that learners receive the support they need to succeed.

6.7 Gamification and Rewards

Gamification is the application of game elements, such as points, badges, and leaderboards, to non-game contexts, like training. Gamified learning experiences add an element of fun and competition, motivating learners to actively participate and excel. Additionally, rewards and recognition for completing training milestones can further boost learner engagement and satisfaction.

6.8 Virtual Instructor-Led Training (VILT)

Virtual Instructor-Led Training (VILT) combines the benefits of face-to-face instruction with the flexibility of online learning. Through web conferencing platforms, instructors can deliver live training sessions, conduct discussions, and engage with learners in real-time. VILT offers a more interactive and collaborative learning experience compared to traditional webinars.

6.9 Conclusion

Technology has revolutionized the field of training and development, offering innovative solutions to enhance training effectiveness and evaluation. From Learning Management Systems (LMS) to virtual reality simulations and data analytics, organizations have a wealth of tools at their disposal to create engaging, personalized, and data-driven learning experiences.

By harnessing the power of technology, organizations can optimize their training programs, measure learning outcomes more effectively, and achieve higher levels of success in their journey towards creating a skilled and knowledgeable workforce.

In the following chapters, we will explore additional aspects of instructional design and evaluation, including strategies for designing engaging learning experiences and addressing common challenges faced during the implementation of the Kirkpatrick Model. Let us continue our exploration of instructional design excellence in the digital age.

Chapter 7 - Designing Engaging Learning Experiences

In Chapter 6, we discussed the role of technology in enhancing training effectiveness. Now, in Chapter 7, we focus on the importance of designing engaging learning experiences. Engaging learning experiences are essential for capturing learners' attention, promoting active participation, and ultimately, driving successful learning outcomes.

7.1 Incorporate Active Learning Strategies

Active learning strategies encourage learners to be actively involved in the learning process rather than passively receiving information. Examples of active learning include group discussions, case studies, hands-on exercises, role-playing, and problem-solving activities. By engaging learners in these interactive experiences, they can apply knowledge in real-life scenarios and retain information more effectively.

7.2 Use Multimedia Elements

Multimedia elements, such as videos, images, animations, and audio, add depth and variety to training content. Visual and auditory aids not only make the learning experience more enjoyable but also cater to different learning styles. Well-designed multimedia can simplify complex concepts and increase learners' comprehension and retention.

7.3 Provide Real-World Relevance

Making the training content relevant to learners' real-world experiences and job roles enhances engagement. When learners see the practical applications of the knowledge and skills they are acquiring, they are more motivated to actively participate in the learning process. Incorporating real-world examples and case studies can bridge the gap between theory and practice.

7.4 Foster Collaborative Learning

Promoting collaborative learning environments fosters teamwork and peer support. Group activities, discussions, and team projects encourage learners to share ideas, exchange perspectives, and learn from one another. Collaborative learning also builds a sense of community among learners, making the training experience more enjoyable and impactful.

7.5 Offer Immediate Feedback

Timely feedback is crucial for learner progress and motivation. Provide learners with immediate feedback on assessments and activities, acknowledging correct answers and offering guidance for incorrect responses. Constructive feedback helps learners understand their strengths and areas for improvement, promoting continuous learning and growth.

7.6 Gamify the Learning Experience

As mentioned in Chapter 6, gamification adds an element of fun and competition to training programs. By incorporating gamified elements, such as points, badges, and rewards, learners are motivated to achieve set goals and excel in their learning journey. Gamification can create a sense of achievement and drive learner engagement.

7.7 Personalize Learning Paths

Customizing learning paths based on individual learner needs and preferences ensures relevance and effectiveness. Utilize adaptive learning technologies to tailor content and assessments according to learners' strengths and weaknesses. Personalized learning paths cater to learners' unique requirements, making the training experience more impactful and efficient.

7.8 Encourage Reflection and Application

Encourage learners to reflect on their learning experiences and apply their newfound knowledge and skills in practical scenarios. Reflection helps reinforce learning and fosters a deeper understanding of the subject matter. Additionally, providing opportunities for learners to apply what they have learned in real-life situations reinforces the training's value.

7.9 Conclusion

Designing engaging learning experiences is a cornerstone of effective instructional design. By incorporating active learning strategies, multimedia elements, real-world relevance, and collaborative activities, instructional designers can create transformative learning experiences that captivate learners' attention and lead to meaningful outcomes.

In the following chapters, we will explore how to address challenges in implementing the Kirkpatrick Model, the importance of continuous improvement, and future trends in instructional design and evaluation. Let us continue our journey of unlocking the full potential of instructional design and creating impactful learning experiences.

Chapter 8 - Addressing Challenges in Implementing the Kirkpatrick Model

In Chapter 7, we discussed the importance of designing engaging learning experiences. Now, in Chapter 8, we shift our focus to the challenges that organizations may encounter when implementing the Kirkpatrick Model for training evaluation. While the model offers valuable insights, its successful implementation requires overcoming certain obstacles.

8.1 Time and Resource Constraints

One of the primary challenges in implementing the Kirkpatrick Model is the allocation of sufficient time and resources for evaluation. Conducting evaluations at multiple levels requires careful planning, data collection, and analysis. Limited resources and time constraints may hinder organizations from conducting comprehensive evaluations, leading to incomplete insights into training effectiveness.

8.2 Identifying Relevant Metrics

Choosing the most appropriate evaluation metrics that align with learning objectives can be challenging. Organizations must identify key performance indicators

(KPIs) that reflect the desired outcomes of the training. Without well-defined and relevant metrics, evaluating the impact of training at higher levels, such as Level 3 (Behavior) and Level 4 (Results), becomes difficult.

8.3 Data Collection and Analysis

Collecting and analyzing data from evaluations can be a complex process. It requires the use of reliable data collection methods, ensuring data accuracy, and employing suitable data analysis techniques. The abundance of data can also be overwhelming, making it essential for organizations to focus on relevant data points that provide meaningful insights.

8.4 Translating Evaluation Results into Action

Even with valuable evaluation data, organizations must be prepared to translate the results into actionable improvements. Identifying areas for enhancement is only effective if steps are taken to address them. Organizations should foster a culture of continuous improvement and use evaluation results as a basis for refining training programs and instructional design.

8.5 Engaging Stakeholders

Obtaining buy-in from stakeholders is crucial for successful training evaluation. Engaging key stakeholders, including senior management, department heads, and supervisors, ensures their support and commitment to the evaluation process. Communicating the value of training evaluation in terms of organizational success can help secure stakeholder involvement.

8.6 Addressing Learner Resistance

In some cases, learners may resist evaluation activities, such as assessments and surveys. Overcoming learner resistance requires transparent communication about the purpose and benefits of evaluation. Organizations should emphasize that evaluation is not about judgment but rather about enhancing the learning experience and ensuring its effectiveness.

8.7 Integrating Evaluation into Training Design

Embedding evaluation into the instructional design process from the outset can be a challenge. Evaluation plans should be established during the initial stages of training development to ensure alignment with learning objectives and seamless data collection. Retroactively implementing evaluation measures may lead to data gaps and missed opportunities for improvement.

8.8 Balancing Qualitative and Quantitative Data

Both qualitative and quantitative data are valuable for comprehensive evaluation. Striking the right balance between the two is essential. While quantitative data offers measurable insights, qualitative data provides deeper context and understanding. Combining both types of data provides a holistic view of training effectiveness.

8.9 Conclusion

Addressing challenges in implementing the Kirkpatrick Model is essential to derive meaningful insights from training evaluation. By proactively planning for evaluation, identifying relevant metrics, and engaging stakeholders, organizations can overcome these challenges and optimize their training programs.

In the following chapters, we will explore the significance of continuous improvement in training and development and examine future trends in instructional design and evaluation. Let us continue our exploration of best practices in creating effective and impactful learning experiences.

Chapter 9 - The Significance of Continuous Improvement in Training and Development

In Chapter 8, we discussed the challenges in implementing the Kirkpatrick Model. Now, in Chapter 9, we focus on the significance of continuous improvement in training and development. Embracing a culture of continuous improvement is vital for organizations to enhance the effectiveness of their training programs and ensure they remain relevant in a rapidly evolving world.

9.1 Emphasizing Feedback and Evaluation

Feedback and evaluation serve as the backbone of continuous improvement. Organizations should actively seek feedback from learners, trainers, and stakeholders to identify areas for enhancement. Regular evaluation, as per the Kirkpatrick Model, allows organizations to measure the impact of training initiatives and make data-driven decisions for improvement.

9.2 Encouraging Collaboration and Learning Communities

Creating a collaborative learning environment fosters knowledge-sharing and encourages employees to learn from one another. Establishing learning communities, where individuals can exchange ideas and best practices, facilitates continuous learning and professional growth. Peer-to-peer learning complements formal training and contributes to skill development.

9.3 Analyzing Training Data and Trends

Data analytics plays a vital role in continuous improvement efforts. Organizations should analyze training data to identify trends and patterns. By scrutinizing learner performance, engagement metrics, and training outcomes, organizations gain insights into the effectiveness of their training programs and can make informed adjustments.

9.4 Leveraging Technology for Agility

Incorporating technology into training and development processes enhances agility and adaptability. Utilizing learning management systems (LMS) and e-learning platforms allows organizations to quickly update training content, respond to changing needs, and deliver personalized learning experiences. Technology enables swift adjustments to training initiatives to keep pace with industry trends.

9.5 Implementing Actionable Feedback Loops

Creating feedback loops ensures that evaluation data leads to actionable improvements. Once evaluation results are obtained, organizations should proactively analyze the data and design action plans to address identified gaps. Regularly closing the loop by implementing these improvements drives continuous progress.

9.6 Investing in Professional Development

Supporting continuous improvement involves investing in the professional development of trainers and learning designers. Equipping these individuals with the latest instructional design methodologies and emerging technologies empowers them to create cutting-edge and impactful learning experiences.

9.7 Promoting a Growth Mindset

Instilling a growth mindset within the organization encourages employees to embrace challenges and view failures as opportunities for learning and improvement. A growth mindset fosters a culture where individuals are motivated to continuously develop their skills and seek out new knowledge.

9.8 Monitoring Industry Trends

Keeping abreast of industry trends and best practices is essential in staying ahead of the curve. Organizations should monitor advancements in instructional design, technology, and learning methodologies to ensure their training programs remain relevant and effective.

9.9 Conclusion

Continuous improvement is the cornerstone of successful training and development initiatives. By emphasizing feedback and evaluation, promoting collaboration, leveraging technology, and nurturing a growth mindset, organizations can create a culture of learning excellence. Embracing continuous improvement ensures that training programs remain impactful, adaptable, and capable of driving positive organizational outcomes.

In the following chapters, we will explore future trends in instructional design and evaluation, providing insights into the evolving landscape of learning and development. Let us continue our journey of unlocking the full potential of training and development practices in the modern era.

Chapter 10 - Future Trends in Instructional Design and Evaluation

In Chapter 9, we explored the significance of continuous improvement in training and development. Now, in Chapter 10, we shift our focus to the future and examine emerging trends in instructional design and evaluation. As technology continues to advance and learning methodologies evolve, organizations must stay at the forefront of these trends to deliver innovative and effective learning experiences.

10.1 Immersive Learning with Extended Reality (XR)

Extended Reality (XR), which encompasses Virtual Reality (VR), Augmented Reality (AR), and Mixed Reality (MR), is poised to revolutionize learning experiences. XR technologies offer immersive simulations and interactive scenarios, providing learners with realistic and hands-on training. From medical simulations to complex machinery operation, XR has the potential to transform how skills are taught and assessed.

10.2 Adaptive Learning and AI-Powered Personalization

Artificial Intelligence (AI) is driving a new era of personalized learning experiences. Adaptive learning platforms use AI algorithms to analyze learner performance and preferences, tailoring content and assessments accordingly. AI-powered chatbots and virtual tutors provide instant support and feedback, enhancing learners' engagement and knowledge retention.

10.3 Microlearning for Continuous Learning

Microlearning, delivering content in short and focused bursts, is gaining momentum in the corporate world. With shrinking attention spans and the need for just-in-time information, microlearning offers learners quick access to targeted knowledge and skills. Organizations are leveraging microlearning to facilitate continuous learning and performance support.

10.4 Gamification for Enhanced Engagement

Gamification will continue to play a significant role in motivating learners and driving engagement. Gamified learning experiences integrate game mechanics, rewards, and competition into training programs. By transforming training into an enjoyable and competitive activity, gamification fosters a sense of achievement and encourages learners to reach their full potential.

10.5 Learning Analytics and Big Data Insights

Learning analytics and big data insights offer organizations a wealth of information on learner behavior, progress, and performance. Data-driven decision-making becomes more refined as organizations analyze vast amounts of learning data. Predictive analytics can help identify potential training gaps and recommend personalized learning paths.

10.6 Social and Collaborative Learning Platforms

Social learning platforms provide opportunities for learners to connect, share knowledge, and collaborate. Online discussion forums, social media groups, and virtual learning communities enable peer-to-peer learning and foster a sense of belonging. Social and collaborative learning platforms facilitate continuous learning beyond formal training sessions.

10.7 Virtual Instructor-Led Training (VILT) Evolution

Virtual Instructor-Led Training (VILT) will continue to evolve with advancements in technology. VILT sessions will become more interactive and immersive, utilizing breakout rooms for group activities, virtual whiteboards for collaborative brainstorming, and enhanced audience engagement tools.

10.8 Blockchain for Credentials and Certifications

Blockchain technology offers a secure and decentralized system for verifying credentials and certifications. Organizations can issue digital certificates on the blockchain, providing learners with portable and tamper-proof credentials that are easily shareable with potential employers or collaborators.

10.9 Conclusion

As we look to the future, instructional design and evaluation are undergoing significant transformations. Embracing emerging trends such as XR technologies, AI-powered personalization, microlearning, and gamification, organizations can create engaging and impactful learning experiences.

By harnessing the power of learning analytics and social learning platforms, organizations can adapt to the evolving needs of learners and facilitate continuous improvement. As the landscape of learning and development continues to evolve, staying informed and agile in adopting these trends will be key to ensuring a successful and future-ready learning ecosystem.

In the final chapter, we will summarize the key takeaways and reinforce the value of instructional design and evaluation in creating a skilled and thriving workforce. Let us conclude our journey of exploration and innovation in training and development practices.

Chapter 11 - Empowering a Skilled and Thriving Workforce

In this final chapter, we will summarize the key takeaways from our exploration of instructional design and evaluation. Empowering a skilled and thriving workforce is at the heart of effective training and development practices. By embracing best practices, leveraging technology, and continuously improving training programs, organizations can unlock the full potential of their employees and drive success.

11.1 Key Takeaways

The Kirkpatrick Model: The Kirkpatrick Model provides a comprehensive framework for evaluating training effectiveness at four distinct levels: Reaction, Learning, Behavior, and Results. Each level contributes unique insights into the impact of training on learners and the organization.

Designing Engaging Learning Experiences: Incorporating active learning strategies, multimedia elements, and real-world relevance creates engaging learning experiences that foster knowledge retention and practical application.

Continuous Improvement: Emphasizing feedback, collaboration, and data analysis allows organizations to continuously enhance their training programs and remain adaptable in a dynamic business landscape.

Technology Advancements: Leveraging emerging technologies like XR, AI, and gamification transforms learning experiences, making them more immersive, personalized, and impactful.

Data-Driven Decision-Making: Learning analytics and big data insights provide organizations with valuable information to make data-driven decisions and tailor learning experiences to individual learner needs.

Social and Collaborative Learning: Building learning communities and fostering social learning platforms promote knowledge-sharing, peer support, and continuous learning.

Future Trends: Staying informed about future trends in instructional design and evaluation is crucial for organizations to stay ahead and create cutting-edge learning experiences.

11.2 The Value of Training and Development

Investing in training and development is not just about acquiring new skills; it's about cultivating a culture of continuous growth and improvement. A skilled and thriving workforce directly impacts an organization's performance, productivity, and innovation.

Effective training initiatives empower employees to:

- Enhance Performance: By acquiring new skills and knowledge, employees become more proficient in their roles, leading to increased productivity and efficiency.

- Boost Morale and Engagement: Training opportunities signal that the organization values its employees' professional growth, fostering a positive and motivated work environment.

- Drive Innovation: Continuous learning encourages employees to think creatively and embrace new ideas, driving innovation and problem-solving.

- Adapt to Change: In a rapidly changing world, skilled employees can adapt quickly to new challenges and industry trends.

11.3 The Journey of Excellence

Instructional design and evaluation are not static processes; they are journeys of excellence. By continuously refining training programs, embracing new technologies, and nurturing a learning culture, organizations can create a workforce that is equipped to meet current and future challenges.

As we conclude this exploration, let us remember that investing in training and development is an investment in the future success of the organization and its people. Let us embark on this journey together, unlocking the full potential of training and development practices, and empowering a skilled and thriving workforce that can shape a brighter tomorrow.

Glossary

Book Chapters:

- Introduction to Instructional Design

- Understanding the Kirkpatrick Model

- The Four Levels of Evaluation

- Level 1: Reaction - Capturing Learner Feedback

- Level 2: Learning - Assessing Knowledge and Skill Acquisition

- Level 3: Behavior - Measuring Application of Learning

- Level 4: Results - Evaluating Organizational Impact

- Applying the Kirkpatrick Model in Real-World Scenarios

- Best Practices in Instructional Design

- Enhancing Training Effectiveness through Technology

- Designing Engaging Learning Experiences

- Measuring Training ROI (Return on Investment)

- Addressing Challenges in Implementing the Kirkpatrick Model

- Continuous Improvement and Iterative Design

- Future Trends in Instructional Design and Evaluation